PRAISE FOR *WILD, WILL...*

"A must-read for anyone seeking inner wisdom and greater self-love."
—**LEISA PETERSON, author of *The Mindful Millionaire***

"A ride on the river of life that is as wild, willful, and crazy-wise as her title promises." —**ROBERT MOSS, bestselling author of *Conscious Dreaming* and *Dreaming the Soul Back Home***

"A much-needed antidote to the heaviness of our current moment in history!" —**VICKI NOBLE, cocreator of Motherpeace Tarot, author of *Shakti Woman*, healer, and international teacher**

"Profound and accessible . . . a must-read!"
—**BANAFSHEH SAYYAD, founder, Dance of Oneness**

"Authentic, life-beautifying guidance." —**DON OSCAR MIRO-QUESADA, author of *Lessons in Courage* and *Common Sentience: Shamanism***

"Beautifully articulated [and] dynamic." —**LINDA STAR WOLF, author of *Shamanic Breathwork* and founder of Venus Rising**

"A wondrous, honest, and confronting journey along the river of life."
—**MICHELLE MACEWAN, Wild Wisdom**

"Delightfully irreverent and yet deeply spiritual."
—**PEGGY DYLAN, author of *Femme Vital!***

"A well-thought-out, process-oriented workbook that takes you from unawareness to profound 'ah-ha's!'" —**SHERI ROSENTHAL, author of *The Complete Idiot's Guide to Toltec Wisdom* and *Banish Mind Spam***

WILD,

WILLING,

AND WISE

ALSO BY HEATHERASH AMARA

The Warrior Heart Practice: A Simple Process to Transform Confusion into Clarity and Pain into Peace

Warrior Goddess Training: Become the Woman You Are Meant to Be

The Seven Secrets to Healthy, Happy Relationships
(with don Miguel Ruiz Jr.)

WILD,

WILLING,

AND WISE

AN INTERACTIVE GUIDE FOR WHEN TO PADDLE,
WHEN TO REST, AND WHEN TO JUMP NAKED
INTO THE RIVER OF LIFE

HEATHERASH AMARA

ST. MARTIN'S
ESSENTIALS
NEW YORK

First published in the United States by St. Martin's Essentials, an imprint of St. Martin's Publishing Group

www.stmartins.com

Designed by Steven Seighman

The Library of Congress Cataloging-in-Publication Data is available upon request.

ISBN 978-1-250-22687-7 (trade paperback)
ISBN 978-1-250-34515-8 (ebook)

Our books may be purchased in bulk for promotional, educational, or business use. Please contact your local bookseller or the Macmillan Corporate and Premium Sales Department at 1-800-221-7945, extension 5442, or by email at MacmillanSpecialMarkets@macmillan.com.

First Edition: 2024

10 9 8 7 6 5 4 3 2 1

To the dreamers who dare to envision
a more just and beautiful world

CONTENTS

WILD,

WILLING,

AND WISE

THIS BOOK IS FOR YOU IF

You want to LIVE in this world . . . to be fiercely engaged, wildly
creative, unfailingly experimental, wonderfully confused, seriously
delighted, and compassionately vulnerable.

You are ready to throw your arms up and embrace this ride of an
embodied, real life and gain the skills for navigating it.

And now, a warning.

WARNING AND AGREEMENT

Proceed with caution, dear ones . . .
I invite you to review and sign the following hella serious
agreement before you go any further with this book.
I, _____, do hereby read and agree with the following:

1. I will do my best to NOT use the writings in this, or any other book, against myself. This means I will refrain from comparing, punishing, or criticizing myself or others based on what I am learning. I will not believe my unkind, judgy inner voice and will tell my critical mind to chill. I will also refrain from using the following pages to shittily judge anyone else.

2. I understand that the information contained in this book is intended as a useful model and a helpful guide, not a dogmatic, rigid, all-knowing tome that I must fit myself into in order to be "good" or "healed." I will refrain from creating more rules and instead use this book to dismantle, dissolve, and bring in more inner freedom, powerful play, and creative action.

3. I agree that there is no one way to use this book. There is only what works for me, which might change, and for which I grant myself permission in advance. I give myself permission to do all the exercises in order, do none of the exercises, or only do the exercises that speak to me.

Signature _____ Date _____

A STORY ABOUT A LITERAL BIG FUCKING RIVER

"Wait a minute. Are those eighteen-foot waves?" I asked, turning to my then husband with the word *WHAT?!* screaming from my eyes.

"Yup," he affirmed, casually smiling at me. He was showing me a video of what I had unknowingly signed myself up for.

Holy fuck.

It was the summer of 2005, and I was about to raft the Grand Canyon with my husband, his father, and a small group of longtime river rats (as they called themselves).

To date, I had been on exactly one trip down a river, when I enthusiastically agreed to join my then fiancé to raft the Arkansas River in Colorado. Mid-rapids, however, we discovered that his old blow-up kayak had a hole.

I was not impressed.

We were about to spend two weeks on a river that can eat boats and occupants in a single bite.

I put the huge waves out of my head. I was with two experts. What could go wrong?

(Cue laughter track from the universe here.)

Before the journey, we spent days planning meals, gathering needed equipment, and studying the Grand Canyon river map, which pinpoints and describes each rapid and helpfully offers suggestions on how to survive.

We entered the river at Lee's Ferry. For the first few days, I was soothed by the wild beauty and sweet ease of being on the river. Smooth water carried us quietly for miles. I watched dragonflies kissing their own reflections and spent hours looking for faces in the cliffs and clouds. The most work I did was getting sunburned.

Even with so many experts and a map to tell us of upcoming rapids, we were lulled by the soft, gentle lapping.

Then the first disaster happened.

One moment, I was contentedly watching the ripples my paddle made in the water, and the next, I was wondering about the poor person making such awful, dying-cat noises as they struggled to breathe.

It took me a few seconds before I realized that that person was me. As I was slammed back into my body, water churned over and around me, so cold I couldn't get air into my lungs. Each short, scared inhale sounded like a teapot whistling next to the dying cat; each exhale was a whimper. The life vest kept my head above water, but I was moving so fast and I was so tiny in this vast flow that I couldn't make sense of anything.

And then I remembered about my husband and father-in-law. Were they okay?

I panicked anew.

I managed to turn around and see the distant shape of my husband's head and shoulders, his arm pointing right. *Of course. Swim to shore.*

I angled my body toward the cliffs and started kicking and flapping my arms, clawing my way into shallower waters.

Finally, I reached solid, blessed land.

Later, when the shaking stopped and we were finally warm and dry around a fire, we reviewed what happened.

It was a tiny rapid, a short stretch of three- to five-foot waves. The last wave playfully slapped the back edge of the boat with just enough force to send us all flying into the air like birds and then plummeting into the water like rocks.

This was day three of our journey. There were eleven days to go, with many more rapids and the looming presence of Lava.

Lava is the name of the grandmama of all rapids on this section of the Colorado River. It was she on the video my husband showed me before our journey, the one with the eighteen-foot waves. Even the seasoned, gray-haired river rats talked about her in an almost worshipful whisper.

I spent the next ten days learning how to read the river. Gone was the previous casual confidence. We consulted the maps every evening to see what was coming. We pulled the boats out of the water and scouted before almost every rapid.

We knew that even with all our study and scouting that the river is mysterious, powerful, and in charge. All we could do was be as prepared as possible, ready for the unexpected.

LAVA DAY

By Lava day, I was stronger, more confident on the river, and had developed a deep respect for who was actually in charge here.

By now, I knew several things:

1. The only way out is through.
2. Being an expert is helpful, but it doesn't mean you won't capsize.
3. Take it slow, look where you are going, make a plan. Scout.
4. Surrender to the flow.
5. We are all in this together.
6. Good guides make everything better.

After Lava, I added another one to my list: 7. Don't jump out of the boat when the going gets tough.

My eyes had grown keener as I started to understand the flow and dance of water, rock, elevation, and canyon width. The biggest rapids happen when elevation drops quickly or the canyon walls narrow. The flow in front of big rocks can pin your boat with thousands of pounds of water; the watery holes after big rocks can suck your boat under without a thought. The waves can shift direction so quickly that going too slow through a rapid, going too fast, or getting turned at an angle can all mean that in a fraction of a second you are in the water instead of in the boat. Eddies and whirlpools and hidden rocks can snag or slow or sink your vessel. Sometimes there is only one path through a rapid; other times there are multiple choices of how to navigate.

We had studied the now-tattered map and knew that the way through Lava was along the right side. As we approached, the roar of water made talking, or even thinking, impossible. We rowed to shore, pulled the boats out of the water, and hiked up the steep rocks so we could see the rapid clearly from above.

This part of the Colorado River is about sixty feet across, and the elevation drops steeply. In the middle of the river is a twenty-foot rock with a fifteen-foot drop behind it and a whirlpool big enough to easily disappear a school bus. To the left of the school-bus-disappearing rock are so many rocks and rapids, which render this side impassable.

To the right is one thin possibility that demands hitting the entrance into the rapid at just the right place, staying between a series of rock sentinels, and then halfway through paddling hard on the left to keep from getting pulled into the big-rock whirlpool.

The final ten or so waves are those mother mountain ones, and the only way through is to keep paddling up the wave so you have enough force to break through the top and ride the crest down to the next one.

As those from our boat watched from our scouting spot, the first boat in our group hit a wave and flipped over, scattering people and oars like marbles bouncing off a table. I looked around and wondered if there was any way I could climb out of the canyon instead of going through Lava.

But that opportunity had passed miles ago. The only way out was through.

We had rehearsed the pathway so many times: staring at the map, reviewing our plan over meals, and now while staring down at Lava from a distance. But as we entered the wide mouth of Lava, I realized NOTHING could have prepared me for this reality.

The sound and spray of rushing water made it feel like we were surrounded by three Niagara Falls turned at fantastical angles. It was a roller coaster without rails.

Paddle right! Stop! Paddle left hard!

About halfway through Lava, I was convinced we were going over. We were airborne for so long, water pounding everywhere, that my body dove for the side, terrified of getting pinned under the boat.

Out of the corner of his eye, my father-in-law saw my diving shape, grabbed my ankle, and pulled me back into the boat.

"It's okay!" he shouted. "Keep rowing!"

I kept rowing.

And then we were through the last big wave, laughing and howling and high-fiving our oars.

WE DID IT!

Three seconds later, we were paddling hard on the left to help the crew that flipped before us, and to be ready for the next boat to traverse Lava.

And the river kept flowing.

HI, FELLOW TRAVELER, SO GLAD YOU ARE HERE

Welcome to the river of life.

Sometimes the water is smooth and sweet, sometimes stagnant and smelly, sometimes frightening and sinister. Yup, that is life. A churning, unpredictable mix of beauty, brutality, benevolence, and broken bits.

Whether you are:

- centered in your being and enjoying the ride
- huddled on the shore unwilling to take part
- frantically trying to save everyone else in the water (except yourself)
- flailing in the choppy, rocky waters and feeling like you are drowning

Or all of the above, you multidimensional being . . .

I see you.

This book is a manual to help you to align with the energy of the river of life and flow with it.

What this is not is a manual to align with life the way you think it should be. Instead, together we will explore life as a river that constantly moves, changes, and creates new pathways. We will tap into the power of letting go. Because when we stop trying to force the river to flow how we think it should, we gain the energy, resources, and vision to flow through the stills and the rapids alike.

I will introduce you to the three energy guides, Wild, Willing, and Wise, to help you know when to put down your oars and rest in the smoother waters and when to pick them up and paddle like hell through the rapids. They will show you how to explore the waters of life (Wild energy), support yourself through the rocky, churning waters (Willing energy), and let your past provide momentum rather than being a damn anchor (Wise energy). And I'll say this one more time so that your beautiful self can really take it in: there is no right or wrong way to use this book. I promise. I'll share a transformational framework, introduce you to some new guides (who may not be so new to some of you), and offer up simple exercises, visualizations, and ponderings to help you access more inner freedom, powerful play, and creative action.

Before entering into the rest of the book, set aside ten minutes to reflect on what it means to you to be wild, willing, and wise. What are you most interested in having more of and why?

BEING WHERE YOU ARE . . .

For this first exercise/step, let's acknowledge where you are. You can't get started on the journey if you don't know where you're departing from!

Whether you feel like you are drowning or flowing in this moment, you are welcome here. You are invited to find your true inner guidance.

So many of us are exhausted, frustrated, and stretched thin by trying to be the "perfect" person: strong, confident, and whole. But this image of perfection is an illusion that keeps us trapped in comparisons and power struggles, not-enoughness, and toxic criticism. For the times we are in, we must learn how to stay aware, brave, and compassionate about what is going on within ourselves and the world around us.

Have you ever tried attacking water with your illusionary sword of productivity or safety or spirituality?

Damn that water. It won't behave, will it? And, beloveds, the truth is that life, other people, and even our bodies don't behave like we would like them to. While we often envision strength as easily chopping through fears and obstacles with a sharp sword of determination, that is a limited, narrow view. The belief that chopping and severing what we don't like or need is the only way through life is damaging to our relationships, health, and creativity. This is not aligning with life but cutting down life, and ourselves, to conform to unrealistic standards of perfection.

Together we will explore, dismantle, and reimagine what it means to be strong. We'll find the power of true tenderness and the promise of grounded sustainability. We will reclaim our full heart-centered self and make a conscious, clear choice to honor the river of life. We will practice the energetic and emotional skills to ride its waves and rest into the sweet lulls. And we will begin exactly where we are.

WHAT IS YOUR CURRENT RELATIONSHIP TO THE RIVER OF LIFE?

Which statements feel most true for you at this time?

0 = Doesn't feel true at all
5 = This is my daily mantra

Be honest, dear traveler of the inner realms.

_____The fucking river should just do exactly what I want it to.
_____I have no power over the river. I am helpless.
_____If I am just one with the river, I will feel no bad things and I'll just be happy.
_____If I keep swimming upstream, I'll get there, damn it!
_____I have to save everyone in this river!

0–5: You are a river of life badass!
6–10: Paddling with one oar is hard.
11–15: You are paddling upriver, sweetheart.
16–25: Let's get you back in the boat.

What do you think your score is telling you?

_____

_____

_____

_____

_____

_____

_____

_____

_____

_____

_____

_____

_____

_____

_____

_____

_____

_____

_____

Intuitively, what do you think you need to be a river-of-life badass?

_____

_____

_____

_____

_____

_____

_____

_____

_____

_____

_____

_____

_____

_____

_____

_____

_____

_____

LESSONS FROM THE RIVER

Now that we have our initial relationship-to-the-river scores, let's take a closer look at what the river really is.

There is nothing quite like a river that is over five million years old moving at fifteen thousand cubic feet per second to remind you who's really boss. And to highlight the importance of getting your shit together for the ride.

Because the river doesn't give a damn who you are or what you have done.

The river is also not out to get you; it is just doing its thing. So whenever you find yourself struggling or sinking, remember this:

Life is a river.

It is flowing, flowing, flowing.

There will be incredible beauty.

There will be rocks.

There will be eddies.

There will be tranquil waters.

There will be holy-Mother-of-God waves.

No matter your skill, sometimes you will capsize.

Others will capsize, too.

So the first thing for us to get straight is this:

Like the river, life has been flowing for a long-ass time and is bigger than all of us tiny humans. We can argue with this fact, try to control the river of life, or give up and spend our lives feeling like we are drowning.

Or we can put on our best adventure shoes, gather our courage, and learn to flow with it. Because, as the first lesson from the river states, the only way out is through.

1. **THE ONLY WAY OUT IS THROUGH.**

The choice you have in this life is whether you are going to be in the adventure or spend your precious life-force energy paddling upstream or trying to scale impossible cliffs.

2. **BEING AN EXPERT IS HELPFUL, BUT IT DOESN'T MEAN YOU WON'T CAPSIZE.**

Nothing, apart from maybe parking yourself on the shore in a self-imposed coma (which will suck even if it seems safe), will prevent you from loss, emotions, or the messiness of life. And no amount of study, meditation, prayer, drugs, or good looks will helicopter you from the beginning to the end. See #1.

3. **TAKE IT SLOW, LOOK WHERE YOU ARE GOING, MAKE A PLAN. SCOUT.**

Let's ditch the drama and instead look where we are going and learn the skills to get there. Gather your supplies for this life journey: clear maps, helpful guides, and nourishing food. Pull up periodically and scout the current territory. Slooooww dowwnnn. Make sure you are well fed and well rested and in this moment.

4. **SURRENDER TO THE FLOW.**

At a certain point, all the planning, thinking, scheming, and visioning must be released with open arms into the mystery. You can't clutch your map as you go through life, yelling that it was wrong. Life doesn't care. Put your arms up, look where you are going, and enjoy the ride. Put your faith in something larger that will guide you when you merge with what is.

5. WE ARE ALL IN THIS TOGETHER.

We all want love and safety and adventure. We want to be seen and appreciated, to have fabulous hair, and to have peace in our hearts. And while we are all in this life together, one truth to remember is that we each have a different type of boat, different skills, and a different history, each of which are helping to buoy us up or weigh us down (or sometimes both, and sometimes at the same time!). Everyone can learn more skills, but remember that we are all starting from different places and perspectives, so we want to bring compassion, patience, and understanding to our beloved cotravelers and to ourselves.

6. GOOD GUIDES MAKE EVERYTHING BETTER.

Imagine if I had decided to go down the Grand Canyon in a boat by myself, with no support, guidance, or skills. Maybe I could have made it through, but it would not have been much fun, and I probably would have spent much of the time wet, hungry, paddling way too much, and missing the beauty of the side canyons and sunshine on the water. Let us always remember that others have traveled before us and we can learn from their wisdom.

7. DON'T JUMP OUT OF THE BOAT WHEN THE GOING GETS TOUGH.

Sometimes when things seem the bleakest, scariest, and most unmanageable is when we are about to break through to the other side. Learn how to stay in the boat and paddle with the current even when you can't see what's next. Because the only way out is through.

RIDING THE RIVER OF LIFE

Now that you are a bit more familiar with the ways of the river of life, put a check mark next to any statement you can relate to in your own life.

1. **The only way out is through.**
   _____I'm going to spend my life avoiding discomfort, conflict, and emotional pain.
   _____I'm not signing up for this.
   _____It's not worth the effort.

2. **Being an expert is helpful, but it doesn't mean you won't capsize.**
   _____If I just read all the books, I'll understand everything.
   _____I can protect myself and others through my sheer willpower.
   _____My worry, anxiety, and worst-case-scenario thinking will save me and my beloveds.

3. **Take it slow, look where you are going, make a plan. Scout.**
   _____There is no time; everything must be done now.
   _____No one can help me. I'm all alone.
   _____Everyone else must help me; I have no power.

4. **Surrender to the flow.**
   _____It's not supposed to be this way.
   _____Life is against me.
   _____Struggle is noble.

5. **We are all in this together.**
   _____They just don't get it. I have to do everything myself.
   _____Other people are unreliable.

_____Hey, it's easy: Just hit the gas on your speedboat through the rapids and stop whining. What, you don't have a speedboat? What is wrong with you?

6. Good guides make everything better.
_____I know better than they do.

_____I don't trust anyone.

_____If I don't do it on my own, it doesn't count.

7. Don't jump out of the boat when the going gets tough.
_____I don't have what it takes.

_____Get me off this ride now.

_____There has got to be another way.

Go back through the statements you checked and pick the three that run through your mind the most often. Write them here:

1. _____

2. _____

3. _____

Now, play with making three new life-affirming statements for yourself. Here's an example:

My three top statements (in no particular order):

1. They just don't get it. I have to do everything myself.

2. I can protect myself and others through my sheer willpower.

3. There is no time; everything must be done now.

My new life-affirming statements:

1. We have so much to learn from each other.
2. I can look where I am going and flow with what is.
3. Paddle, rest. Paddle, rest.

Write your new life-affirming statements here (you can't do it wrong!):

1. _____
2. _____
3. _____

FROM CONCEPT TO EMBODIMENT

Now all you have to do is live your life by those three new statements you just wrote and you will be ready to navigate anything that comes your way with grace, grit, and glee.

Right? Right?

We all wish it were that damn simple.

That's like saying, "But I packed the boat with everything I needed. Why is the river not cooperating with me?"

Remember: life is complicated, unpredictable, and sometimes a real bitch.

And what can make it even harder is that many of the current motivational models of transformation are a wee bit of the masculine, patriarchal, over-the-top-judgmental flavor. Cue someone yelling at you: "JUST PADDLE! YOU ARE NOT PADDLING HARD ENOUGH! ONLY WIMPS DON'T KNOW HOW TO PADDLE!"

Often . . . the one doing the yelling is you. How's that going?

Now imagine, what would a holistic, feminine-informed, deeply healing new paradigm look like?

How can you embody your three life-affirming statements instead of just thinking about them, punishing yourself for not embodying them, or blaming your parents for not raising you right so you could embody them?

Alas, the river is not going to stop.

So let's call in our guides for this wild-ride journey.

YOUR THREE ENERGY GUIDES

The lessons from my river trip down the Grand Canyon continued to reverberate in my being long after the journey was over. As I integrated everything I learned, I realized that in life, like on a river, we need guides—three in particular.

Allow me to introduce you to your support team: Wild, Willing, and Wise.

WILD: our creativity, curiosity, adventurer energy . . . the aspect of us that is innocent and playful and believes that everything is possible.

Our Wild guide is the one who says, "Let's keep going—that was amazing!" after the boat tips over or things get scary.

WILLING: our stabilizing, nourishing, and generative energy . . . the aspect of us that births and raises children, projects, businesses, and communities.

Our Willing guide is the one who keeps us going when the going gets tough and reminds us when to paddle and when to rest.

WISE: our visionary, intuitive, and patient energy . . . the aspect of us that listens deeply and holds the big picture.

Our Wise guide is the one who knows how to surrender and let go into what is, to merge with the river and ride the waves.

While we all carry the energies of Wild, Willing, and Wise within us, for many, they are out of balance. When we are deficient in one energy or relying excessively on one or more, we feel off-kilter, weighed down, uncertain, and unsteady. But when we have all three energies working together in the boat with us, we feel steady and prepared to flow with the river of life. When we can bring these three energies into balance, they are the best outfitted, experienced, and fun guides you could ever ask for.

MEET WILD

Your WILD guide is creative, curious, and adventurous. It is the part of you that's ready to jump into the river and start flowing. It is your inner Wild child. With Wild energy comes a sense of delight and awe and wonder that is already inside each of us, that bone-deep joy of being alive. But often, especially as we flow through life, our Wild energy gets out of balance due to trauma, impetuousness, fear, or stagnation.

- Signs you have too little Wild energy: You'd rather stay on the shore than experience the river of life. You find it hard to see the lighter side of situations. You feel pessimistic about the future.
- Signs you have too much Wild energy: You jump into the river of life without an oar or even a life jacket. You make your decisions on impulse. You frequently make promises you don't keep.

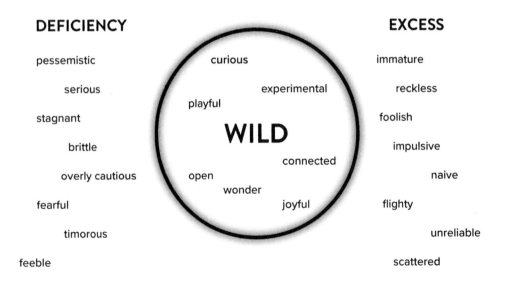

DEFICIENCY

pessemistic

serious

stagnant

brittle

overly cautious

fearful

timorous

feeble

WILD

curious

experimental

playful

connected

open

wonder

joyful

EXCESS

immature

reckless

foolish

impulsive

naive

flighty

unreliable

scattered

When our Wild energy flows naturally, we experience the joy of being alive. We see the world through new, curious eyes. We can bring that childlike wonder and delight in balance in our lives by removing anything that's blocking its flow. And when our Wild tips toward impulsiveness and immaturity, we can gently guide ourselves back toward curious connection.

On the diagram, circle the words under each category that most relate to you. Write down the top three that best describe how you see yourself right now.

1. _____
2. _____
3. _____

Which side of Wild energy are you most aligned with: deficient, centered, or excess? _____

_____
_____
_____
_____
_____

How does Wild energy manifest in your life? _____

_____
_____
_____
_____
_____
_____
_____
_____

What do you think/feel/sense about Wild energy? Write without editing or thinking . . . Just see what comes out of your beautiful brain.

_____

_____

_____

_____

_____

_____

_____

_____

_____

_____

_____

_____

_____

_____

_____

_____

_____

_____

_____

_____

_____

_____

_____

_____

_____

_____

_____

_____

Use your imagination to draw or describe what your inner Wild guide would look like for you at this time. You might be inspired by someone you know, a movie or fictionalized character, or even an animal!

Your WILLING guide is stabilizing, nourishing, and generative. It is the part of you that remembered to bring all the supplies to sustain and nourish you on your journey. It is what you can count on to keep you rowing down the river. Willing energy is most present in the phase of our life when we're actively nurturing and nourishing ourselves and our projects: work, children, our art. While there is a mothering quality to this guide, it isn't about gender or biological fertility. It is about offering our attention and care to ourselves and others.

- Signs you have too little Willing energy: You are ready to jump out of the boat when the river of life gets choppy. You feel frustrated and powerless. You feel like the river just wants to flow against you, so why bother trying?
- Signs you have too much Willing energy: You bring supplies for all the boats and are trying to row them all. You base your value on being of service to others. You feel resentful and exhausted because you've taken on too much.

DEFICIENCY

impotent

anxious

victimized

depressed

hopeless

incomplete

envious

creative

nourishing

sustainable

WILLING

honest

generative

steady

strong

EXCESS

codependent

controlling

angry

judgmental

resentful

drained

unfulfilled

bitter

When our Willing energy flows naturally, we are steady, strong, and mature—we take honest responsibility for our choices without blame or guilt. We can bring our willingness forward by doing the inner work to wash away insecurity, victimization, and anxiety. And when we release codependency and caretaking, we can discover sustainable nourishment and ease.

On the diagram, circle the words under each category that most relate to you. Write down the top three that best describe how you see yourself right now.

1. _____
2. _____
3. _____

Which side of Willing energy are you most aligned with: deficient, centered, or excess? _____

_____
_____
_____
_____
_____

How does Willing energy manifest in your life? _____

_____
_____
_____
_____
_____
_____
_____
_____
_____

What do you think/feel/sense about Willing energy? Write without editing or thinking . . . Just see what comes out of your sweet heart.

Use your imagination to draw or describe what your inner Willing guide would look like for you at this time. It could be inspired by a heroine in your favorite book, a superhero, a marvelous mother figure, or someone you remember from your youth.

MEET WISE

Your WISE guide is visionary, intuitive, and patient. It's the part of you that knows how to use what you've learned from past excursions to go further, safer, and more smoothly down the river of life. Our Wise energy helps us to live our experiences fully and learn from them. When we are seated in our wisdom, we know how to face—rather than avoid or minimize—challenges and loss.

- Signs you have too little Wise energy: You think the river of life has already taught you all that you need to know. You take everything personally. You get stuck in productivity loops and constant doing.
- Signs you have too much Wise energy: Past experiences are weighing down your boat so you can't flow. You immediately reject the new and unfamiliar. You feel the need to control the people and circumstances in your life.

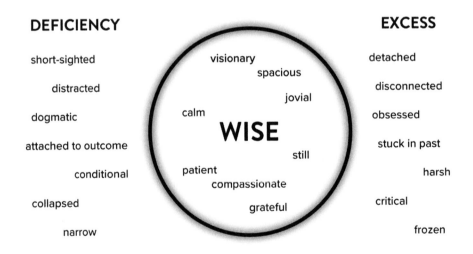

Your Wise energy knows how to step back, get perspective, and see the larger picture. When you have embodied your wisdom, there isn't a sense of "I have to figure this out or fix it." You are paying attention to where you're going, you know where you want to go, and you simply wait for the right moment to make a move so it's effective. Your wisdom is your root, your belly, your womb space, connected to nature, connected to the divine.

On the diagram, circle the words under each category that most relate to you. Write down the top three that best describe how you see yourself right now.

1. _____
2. _____
3. _____

Which side of Wise energy are you most aligned with: deficient, centered, or excess? _____

_____
_____
_____
_____
_____

Share an example of how it manifests in your life. _____

_____
_____
_____
_____
_____
_____

What do you think/feel/sense about Wise energy? _____

_____

_____

_____

_____

_____

_____

_____

_____

_____

_____

_____

_____

_____

_____

_____

_____

_____

_____

_____

_____

_____

_____

_____

_____

_____

_____

Write without editing or thinking . . . Just see what comes out of your belly and hips. _____

_____

_____

_____

_____

_____

_____

_____

_____

_____

_____

_____

_____

_____

_____

_____

_____

_____

_____

_____

_____

_____

_____

_____

_____

_____

_____

_____

_____

_____

_____

Use your imagination to draw or describe what your inner Wise guide would look like for you at this time. It could be inspired by someone who inspired you, a teacher, or a vision of your future self.

PICK A GUIDE

Now that you've been properly introduced to the Wild, Willing, and Wise energies—both in balance and out of balance—it's time to explore how they can help you paddle on the river of life.

Visualizations are a way to help you bypass your thinking I-must-logically-figure-this-out mind (which often means you make decisions based on what you know or who you've been) and tunes you in to your sensing body-based inner guidance (ahh, much better).

Below is a visualization exercise to help you identify the right guide for you in this moment. You can also find an audio recording of this visualization and all the others in this book at wildwillingwise.com.

Think about an issue you are currently navigating. Imagine that you can look at the problem from a little bit of a distance, as if you were seeing it from an eagle-eye point of view. Don't try to fix or change what is happening. Just simply witness it.

Now ask yourself: Which guide—Wild, Willing, or Wise—would be most helpful in this situation?

Breathe into your belly, and do your best to not think or try to figure out what is "right." Let yourself relax and see who comes forward. You might perceive a Wild, Willing, or Wise guide coming up to you. You might have a knowing sensation in your body that you need to access your Wild, Willing, or Wise energy. You might get a message from your Wild, Willing, or Wise self. Be curious, listen, and be open to how the information might come to you.

Listen to the audio for this visualization at wildwillingwise.com/guide.

Which guide—Wild, Willing, or Wise—could you use more of in your life at this time?

WILD   **WILLING**   **WISE**

Jot down any quick insights or questions from your visualization.

_____

_____

_____

_____

_____

_____

_____

_____

_____

_____

_____

_____

_____

_____

_____

_____

_____

_____

_____

_____

_____

_____

_____

_____

_____

SCOUTING YOUR INNER TERRITORY

Take some time to reflect on your visualization from the previous exercise, and then ask yourself which guide would you pick to share a meal with—Wild, Willing, or Wise—and why? _____

_____

_____

_____

_____

_____

_____

_____

Which guide feels most comfortable to you? Why? _____

_____

_____

_____

_____

_____

_____

_____

_____

Which guide feels least comfortable to you? Why? _____

_____

_____

_____

_____

_____

_____

_____

_____

Who, to you, embodies each of the three energies (someone you know or not, alive or not)?:

WILD: _____

_____

WILLING: _____

_____

WISE: _____

_____

Who do you tend to be inspired by as role models: Wild, Willing, or Wise? Why? _____

_____

_____

_____

_____

_____

_____

_____

_____

_____

_____

_____

_____

_____

_____

_____

INTREPID TRAVELERS, REMEMBER

You've just done a lot of reflecting, so it's time to take a pause and integrate the journey so far. At this stage, let's remember . . .
You don't need to:

- beat yourself up or feel bad about where you are . . . just claim your power to do it a different way;
- keep carrying the weight of your past piled high as you bump against rocks and get stuck in eddies;
- fight and struggle and try to fix the river or feel responsible for what others on the river are doing.

The river of life is never going to stop. But you can become a Wild, Willing, and Wise badass who knows how to lean into the rapids when things are rough and lie back in the sunshine when things are calm. With your Wild, Willing, and Wise energies in balance, you will have the fierce focus and heart-centered inspiration to flow with style and grace along the river of life.

In these first pages, we created a map of transformation. Now, you have a bird's-eye view of the territory. You can see and feel the power and beauty of the river in all her manifestations. Next, we will take our conceptual understanding of the river and learn how to embody our inner Wild, Willing, and Wise trinity for when the going gets rough, during transitions, or when we are riding the waves and want to go even further. I'll share more personal water experiences (like the time my Wild almost got me drowned in a raging creek; the dam of tears bursting that helped me finally address my burned-out, caretaking, overactive Willing self; and the big picture of how sometimes what looks like unconscious behavior can actually be Wise).

And everything will become a lot more fun, even the challenges.

So get ready for the next level of how to get your shit together and align with, rather than fight, the flow of life.

So far, we've learned the seven lessons of the river and the importance of respecting yourself in relationship to both the obstacles and the synchronicities of life.

We've gotten familiar with our new guides: the playful, curious Wild; the nourishing and steady Willing; and the patient and intuitive Wise.

Next up: learning the skills to read and respond to the ever-changing flow.

But before we move on, let's do a quick integration exercise. Take five minutes to write, draw, or doodle about what you are taking away from this section of the guide. What has this exploration of your inner territory brought up for you? _____

_____

_____

_____

_____

_____

_____

_____

_____

WILD

I am no bird; and no net ensnares me:
I am a free human being
with an independent will.

—CHARLOTTE BRONTË

To be whole. To be complete. Wildness reminds us what it means to be human, what we are connected to rather than what we are separate from.

—TERRY TEMPEST WILLIAMS

What came to mind as you read these quotes? Write freely and with Wild abandon. _____

_____

_____

_____

_____

_____

_____

_____

_____

_____

_____

_____

_____

_____

_____

_____

_____

_____

_____

_____

_____

_____

_____

_____

_____

SHUTTING DOWN MY WILD

I was thirteen when I firmly closed the door on my wildness.

She was problematic. She felt too deeply, loved too strongly, played too freely. It felt much too dangerous to let her roam untethered in the world. I was safer without her. It felt better to turn toward the protection of being quiet, contained, and armored.

Shutting down my Wild only took a moment; it was a quick calculation of risk and capacity. I chose to be numb, to stop feeling and exploring, in favor of behaving and belonging.

What I didn't understand at the time was how this decision tore and continued for decades to rip me from my authentic, curious, wildly creative self. Instead, I learned to perform being a "proper" young woman—that is, someone who lived to please others.

Instead of listening to my own truth, I tuned in to what others wanted me to be. In favor of being liked, I repressed my voice and values. Given a choice of integrity or making someone else happy, or comfortable, or valued, I almost always chose to act on my perception of what would be the best thing for others.

But the seeds of my Wild weeds were always waiting in the darkness for the moment a crack of light appeared. And so it is with each of us. The Wild will push through even the tiniest space, seeping like water through even the most heavily guarded emotional dams.

So after years of repressing, pushing down, and contorting my Wild self . . . well, as my beloved red mug states:

"Then one day she said fuck this shit and lived happily ever after."

Ahhhh, I wish it had been that easy. It was not. But through questioning, therapy, spiritual work, family healing, living off-grid in a cabin by myself, and learning from other humans, animals, trees, and rivers, I have now fully and fiercely reclaimed my Wild creative self.

And you can, too, no matter how long or strongly you've hidden away your wildness.

Let's walk together, hand in hand, and I'll help you lovingly awaken your Wild creativity, rekindle your passionate, playful fire, and show you how to ally with adventure. Note: I said ally with adventure, not tempt fate, like my friend and I did in the next story.

WHEN WILD BECOMES RECKLESS

I used to live in Austin, Texas, near a waterway called Barton Creek. My girlfriend and I had floated the peaceful Guadalupe River many times, so we assumed Barton Creek would be a fun challenge.

But my husband who was a professional kayak and canoe guide and who understood both the power and the immense danger of water, was not of the same opinion. He shook his head and said, "Don't die. It's really not safe."

First warning: river expert saying it is a bad idea.

The first time we kayaked the creek, it was flowing at around two hundred cubic feet per second (CPS). We thoroughly miscalculated how long it would take us to traverse from our "put-in" point to where we planned to "pull out," as they say in river lingo.

We ended up wet and in the dark, miserably trying to find a place to safely exit the rocky creek. But that wasn't enough to deter us. In fact, we upped the ante considerably.

"The creek is a thousand CPS!" I said on the phone to my friend, ready for a new adventure. "Let's go!"

Second warning: superfast brown, churning water.

We were Wild, and we wanted to play with the wild waters. Our enthusiasm lasted all of five minutes before we realized we were in big trouble.

Third warning: no other kayakers anywhere on Barton Creek.

Even a highly experienced kayaker would have been challenged by these waters (which—surprise!—was why they were all at home waiting for the water level to drop). We, two novices, even with our highly creative, determined, and fearless attitudes, were completely outmatched.

Very ungracefully, I somehow managed to paddle hard enough to make it to the opposite shore about forty feet from where we put in. My friend was not so lucky. She hit a rock and was slammed sideways against it by the force of the water. As her kayak rapidly filled with water, she finally managed to get out. Now she stood chest deep in rushing water, hanging on with one hand to the rope attached to her kayak, which was trying to pull her downstream with it.

"Let go of the kayak!" I yelled to her.

"NO!" she yelled back.

We yelled back and forth at each other for a few minutes. There was no way I could get to her unless she let go of her kayak and used that hand to grab onto my outstretched paddle. She was unwilling to let go of her kayak, which she knew she would never see again.

"YOU ARE MORE IMPORTANT THAN YOUR KAYAK! WE WILL GET YOU ANOTHER ONE!"

With a cry of sorrow, she opened her hand and let go.

And that is how the waters taught me that being Wild does not mean you are invincible.

Have good adventures, Wild one. Learn from them. And don't die.

WILD AWARENESS

Each of us has a story of when we wrestled our Wild into a cage, buried her underground, or relegated her to the closet along with our teddy bears, toys, and too-small clothes.

At other times, we may have done the opposite: hijacked our Wild and pushed her in front of us as a shield against the scary world of adulting.

Getting Wild energy in balance starts with Awareness, a neutral wondering, an exploration of thoughts and emotions from a place of witness. Most of us don't know how to use our Awareness properly. Often our Awareness is swirling in the crowded whirlpools of our feelings, stories, and old hurts. Instead of consciously looking where we are going, we spiral around and around in our anxious, bored, or chaotic minds.

Imagine you're on a river trip. You're spending all your time worried about what rapid or difficult stretch of the water is coming. Even the times of calm waters and blue skies are grayed out by your anxiety about what may come. What if you were so worried, you opted out of the ride entirely? You miss the incredible views, the company of the people you are with, the good food, the experience, and the exhilaration of living.

Now imagine the opposite: you throw yourself into the boat without paying any attention to the weather, the supplies you need, or the rapids coming up. What starts off as exuberant fun ends with you flailing in the water or scaring/endangering other people.

Awareness allows you to clearly perceive both the rapids and the smooth waters ahead.

So our first Wild exercise is to tap into our Awareness so we can see ourselves and the river of life through clear, open, and curious eyes.

WILD VISUALIZATION

Below is the visualization exercise to help you tap into your Wild Awareness. You can also find an audio recording of this visualization and all the others in this book at wildwillingwise.com.

Imagine you are standing facing your future. On one side of you is a crabby, cranky, fearful, brokenhearted, terrified, or repressed kid who only sees disaster, drama, and dreams shattered. Imagine this child is yelling (or whimpering): "YOU SUCK! DON'T BE YOU! YOU HAVE TO BE PERFECT! EVERYONE ELSE KNOWS BETTER! IT'S NOT SAFE!"

On the other side of you is a playful, creative, and curious kid who sees possibility. This child delightfully claps their hands and exuberantly exclaims: "THIS WILL BE FUN! LET'S TRY IT! WHY NOT? YES!"

Which ally are you going to pick to guide you into your next steps?

Now here is the trick: you must choose both.

Hold the hands of both of these kids. BOTH OF THEM ARE PRECIOUS!

Awareness is not about ignoring the "bad," fearful parts of ourselves in favor of the "good," freeing parts of ourselves. Awareness is about acknowledging ALL the parts at play, witnessing them with a sense of humor, and then choosing where to put our attention. While we don't want to be pushed forward by our fears that everything is horrible, we also don't want to be blinded by naivety that everything will be wonderful and without consequence.

Aligning with your Wild is all about playful actions and curious experimentation. Be aware of the risks as well as the old agreements and fears that are trying to snag you. Take fabulous leaps anyway.

Okay. Visualize holding hands with your fears and freedom. Now let's consciously scout the landscape of the Wild self.

Listen to the audio for this visualization at wildwillingwise.com/wild.

Jot down any quick insights or questions from your visualization.

_____

_____

_____

_____

_____

_____

_____

_____

_____

_____

_____

_____

_____

_____

_____

_____

_____

_____

_____

_____

_____

_____

_____

WILD MUSINGS

How do you balance fear and freedom in your life? _____

_____

_____

_____

_____

_____

Recall a time you felt centered in your creative, curious, adventurous
Wild. How did it feel? What supported you in feeling this way? _____

_____

_____

_____

_____

_____

What would help you reclaim that feeling every day? _____

_____

_____

_____

_____

_____

_____

_____

_____

_____

Here are some of the ways you might have smushed or subverted your fire. Put an *X* next to ones that resonate with you.

Note: Remember, detective of love, witness yourself, don't judge! Scout the territory with neutral curiosity.

_____Believing you have to be mature all the time
_____Staying immature so you don't have to take responsibility

_____Thinking being Wild means you get to be reckless and impulsive
with no consequences
_____Being overly cautious and timid for fear of hurting others

_____Being unreliable and flighty, and claiming it is your spiritual path
_____Claiming your brittleness and fear as just the way it is

_____Confusing being impulsive with taking mindful action
_____Confusing being pessimistic with being "real"

_____Using sexuality and pleasure for approval or to avoid feeling alone
_____Closing off your sexuality and pleasure as unimportant or a burden

Review the *X*s on your list above and craft one new agreement that would stoke your Wild fire.

Examples:

I can be mature and playful, free and focused.
I can take mindful action from openhearted curiosity.
My sexuality and pleasure is for me.

Write freely with loving Awareness and no judgment. Get curious.

My new Wild Energy Agreement: _____

_____

_____

_____

_____

_____

_____

_____

_____

_____

_____

_____

_____

_____

_____

_____

_____

_____

_____

_____

_____

_____

_____

_____

_____

_____

_____

_____

_____

_____

WILD AND FREE

Young animals learn through the sheer, unbridled delight of play and experimentation. Connected to our wildness, we, too, can feel supported and free to cavort and cartwheel, growl and giggle, playact the possibilities and ponder the wonders.

Can you feel this Wild fire burning brightly within you?

Wild Qualities

Curious
Playful
Experimental
Connected
Wondrous
Exuberant
Joyful
Spontaneous
Carefree

Which quality above resonates with you right now? Pick one from the list or choose your own. Now, claim it in writing.

I claim being _____.

Think of a recent chaotic or drama-filled situation. How did you respond to it? _____

_____

_____

_____

_____

_____

_____

Imagine yourself as a scout, observing the territory of your life from the shore. For now, take in the information. Discern rather than judge. Explore rather than react. Wonder rather than wail. Be curious rather than crash. Now, consider how your response might have been different if you were to draw on the Wild quality you claimed above.

WILD MEDICINE

Actions to awaken your WILD when you are stuck . . .

Check the ones that appeal to you.

_____Finger-paint with as many colors as possible.

_____Make a cave out of pillows, couch cushions, and blankets.

_____Move your body. Play your three favorite upbeat songs and dance as if no one is watching.

_____Attend a dance class: Nia, ecstatic, ballroom, ballet, jazz . . .

_____Break, tear, or pound something. Safely break dishes, recycled glass, or frozen ice; tear up phone books or paper from your recycle bin; beat on pillows or a mattress with a plastic bat.

_____Make animal sounds, loud and fierce. Add in claws and teeth.

_____Dress up in your fanciest clothes and go get ice cream.

_____Wrap yourself in fuzzy blankets. Pretend you are in a cocoon. Slowly push yourself free and spread your arms, flapping them like wings.

_____Bounce up and down on the balls of your feet, making low noises in your throat.

_____Sit with a fire or a candle flame, and ask Fire to teach you how to shine brightly.

Brainstorm three more ways that you can awaken your Wild energy:

1. _____

2. _____

3. _____

ACTIONS TO REBALANCE YOUR WILD WHEN YOU FEEL OUT OF CONTROL

Check the ones that appeal to you.

_____Go to the grocery store and take your time picking out four fruits. Slow down and connect with the shapes, colors, textures, and fragrance of each fruit. Go home and make a beautiful fruit salad work of art. Then eat it slowly, savoring each flavor.

_____Write an angry letter. Let it all out.

_____Write a poem with your nondominant hand.

_____Consult with a wise friend first before you make any big life changes.

_____Practice pausing numerous times a day and come back into the present moment by taking four deep breaths and feeling your feet on the ground.

_____Spend time with people who are physically slower than you, and match their pace.

_____Ask people close to you how your actions impact them and what would help them trust you more.

_____Practice feeling your impulses without taking any action—breathe deeply and feel your feet on the ground.

_____Commit to being responsible for something: a plant, a puppy, a project.

_____Find a slow, methodical practice that you do weekly: yin yoga, tai chi, chi gong, walking meditation, writing haiku.

Brainstorm three more ways that you can balance your Wild energy:

1. _____

2. _____

3. _____

What name would you give to your Wild guide? It can be anything at all. Just let it come to you without thinking too much (and remember this is *your* Wild—you can change its name at any time!).

My Wild name is: _____.

BONUS: Create a Wild jar. Write down your favorite suggestions from the list above on separate pieces of paper, fold them up, and place them in the jar. If you are feeling creative, decorate and label the jar. When you are needing some Wild medicine, pick one from your jar and just do it!

And don't forget to invite Wild playmates who want to explore with you. Your kids, parents, peers, pets, even strangers can all benefit from more play. Take the risk to ask.

WILD REVIEW

- Wild living is not just for the young. We need the fiery wildness within us burning bright at all ages.
- Dampen your wildness and you dampen your creativity and joy.
- Wild doesn't mean reckless. All actions have consequences.

When you feel out of balance with your Wild:

1. Step back and tap into your Awareness.
2. Scout and assess the territory.
3. Ask your Wild to inspire and ignite your next steps.

Before we move on from Wild to more fully explore our relationship with Willing, give yourself a big hug and maybe shake your body around to celebrate reconnecting and balancing your inner Wild. YES!

Oh darling, your wild and untameable
has been the best part of you all along.
Welcome home.

—NIKKI ROWE

WILLING

The kind of beauty I want most is the
hard-to-get kind that comes from within—
strength, courage, dignity.

—RUBY DEE

Your willingness to look at
your darkness is what
empowers you to change.

—IYANLA VANZANT

What came to mind as you read these quotes? Write freely with an open heart. _____

_____
_____
_____
_____
_____
_____
_____
_____
_____
_____
_____
_____
_____
_____
_____
_____
_____
_____
_____
_____
_____
_____
_____
_____
_____
_____
_____
_____
_____
_____
_____
_____
_____

I DON'T WANT TO . . . AND I AM WILLING

I don't want to I don't want to I don't want to ran like a river through my head.

"Go now!" my friend cheered.

I ran toward the scary ocean (*I don't want to I don't want to*) trusting my friend's guidance (*I don't want to*), ready to dive through the monstrous wave (*I don't want to*) ahead of me.

While I spent my childhood playing in the waters of warm, salty seas, big waves always terrified me. I intimately knew the power of those waves to suck under, roll, and spin the unwary. So while others frolicked, I usually waited in the safe sand or hung out in the shallow foam.

Until my friend Christine noticed my fear. We were in Maui. The waves seemed like four-story buildings.

"Let's go play in the waves!" she called to me. I just shook my head, eyes wide.

Her voice dropped, and she came close to me and said, "You are scared. It's okay. Come on, I'll show you how."

For the next ten minutes, Christine talked me through how to approach big ocean waves. We counted waves. She had me watch for when and how a wave breaks. She gave me options of how to dive through, jump over, or go sideways through a wave.

She was confident but kind, sharing something she loved passionately without being pushy. My body started to relax being around her, and I felt a teeny-tiny bit braver.

When she asked me if I was ready, I thought, *I don't want to. I'm scared.*

But I was Willing, and I did want to.

"I'll be right next to you," she said.

We ran, knees high, over the churning white foam of the previous waves. The ocean grew ahead of me, water becoming horizon, and then sky.

I don't want to I don't want to I don't want to.

I am willing.

"Dive NOW!" Christine yelled.

I made my body an arrow, pushing off the ocean floor and launching myself with a prayer through the solid mass before me. All thought, fear, identity dissolved like tissue paper.

And then we were bobbing gently in the rolling ocean, laughing and hugging on the other side of where the waves break.

I am willing. I am brave. Even when I don't want to be.

WILLING MARTYRDOM

It was a simple correction in a yoga class that unleashed decades of tears and showed me how completely out of balance I had become.

"Bring your shoulder back and open your chest," she said to me, gently putting a hand on my chest and between my shoulder blades as she guided me deeper into the standing twist.

As my chest opened and my left shoulder relaxed, I suddenly found myself weeping. Not nice, polite tears—big, snotty, hiccupy tears that went on and on.

"Keep going," my instructor, Ana Forrest, encouraged me, and I knew she meant, *Keep doing your yoga with us, and keep weeping.*

For the next hour, years of caretaking, fixing, and holding poured out of me in the form of tears. Later, after I had cried myself empty, I was able to look back and see all that I had been holding.

Four years earlier, in 2001, I had started teaching and writing full time. Soon, I started holding multiple classes, traveling to teach workshops, training teachers, and hiring office staff.

I loved what I was doing, but I had no idea how to say one simple word:

No.

I said yes to everything and felt like It was my responsibility to fix, help, and take care of everyone and everything.

If someone called me with a problem, I spent hours on the phone with them, even long past my own capacity to be present. If I thought someone was struggling, even if they didn't ask for help, I would stop my writing or ignore my need for rest and try to fix the issue. If someone on my staff was not feeling well or just wanted to go home early because they were tired, I'd stay up all night working on the website or putting the email together to "help out."

If work wasn't done the way it needed to be, I would not tell the person responsible for it: I would simply go fix it. All of this meant that people leaned more and more heavily on me, and I felt more and more like I needed to control everything around me.

The result? Resentment, exhaustion, and feeling like I had to carry the burden without help.

There was a huge cost for my over-willingness to be what I perceived everyone else needed me to be. But there were also huge benefits.

I avoided conflict and discomfort by focusing on pleasing everyone else.

I got to hold on to my identity of being nice and helpful and kind.

I avoided my own fear of being rejected.

It was easier to focus on everyone else's issues rather than turning to face my own.

In truth, my willingness was a form of panicked doggy-paddling to keep my head, and in my mind everyone else's, above water.

I needed to be willing to let go, to sink underneath the waters of my habits and patterns, and learn to swim in a new way. It meant letting go of the perceived benefits of my excess willingness and realizing that the cost to myself and everyone around me was way too high.

After my teary meltdown, it took years to learn to witness my over-willingness and name it for what it was: trying to take care of every situation and every other person so I felt worthy of love.

Today, I still can slip into taking responsibility for what is not mine to hold. But most of the time, saying no is as easy as saying yes. I know equally how to rest and when to rise to hard occasions. And I am not afraid of being rejected, because I've learned to not reject myself.

I am Willing to rest.

I am Willing to be with my own or other's discomfort.

I am Willing to say no.

I am Willing to pause and wait until I am clear of what the next most beneficial action is.

I am Willing to watch someone else struggle or make mistakes.

I am Willing to face my own fears and vulnerabilities.

I am Willing to not know.

I am Willing to be wrong.

I am Willing to find my inner worth through being rather than doing.

I am Willing.

Caretaking and codependency may feel like love, but they are based in fear. To grow, be willing to let yourself—and others—be uncomfortable. Find new comfort and ease by truly nourishing yourself and others from the heart.

WILLING BRAVERY

Willingness requires taking responsibility for what is ours while respecting and releasing what others are responsible for. This is how we learn to nourish ourselves in a sustainable way, to do hard things not from force but from love.

Imagine if every single time you saw someone or something struggling in the water you jumped out of the boat without a life vest and tried to save them. You wouldn't get very far down the river before you were swallowing water and struggling to keep your own head above the swirling drama.

You may have tied your Willing mojo to a stake of martyrdom, or swore to be always available all the time no matter the cost to you so no one ever feels dropped like you have in the past (basically dropping yourself constantly).

Or you may have done the opposite: become impenetrable, independent, and isolated.

We must be brave enough to face the ways we have focused on taking care of others as a way to avoid taking care of ourselves. Bravery invites us to go toward discomfort so real transformative change can unfold. Bravery is not about forcing, fixing, or forgetting. It is an act of Bravery to simply be with ourselves where we are, to see our beauty and our flaws, and to tend to whatever parts of ourselves need care. Taking care of our own responsibilities and releasing our need to always put others first is what keeps us going steady down that transformative path.

How do we support our Willing energy and ensure we have the fuel we need to keep going?

Through brave, self-nourishing action. And so, our first Willing exercise is to tap into our Bravery so we can face our fears and discomfort about making the choices that keep our own boats upright and flowing down the river.

WILLING VISUALIZATION

Below is the visualization exercise to help you identify what you need to do to keep your own boat advancing down the river. You can also find an audio recording of this visualization and all the others in this book at wildwillingwise.com.

> IMAGINE THIS: *You are riding down the river of life. Your loved ones are in their own boats on their own journeys. It's tiring being on the river—for you and for them. These are your options:*
>
> *You barely have the energy to keep your boat steady; nevertheless, you're trying to guide their boats and help them through this rocky patch.*
>
> *Or you decide it's all too much and you just stop rowing.*
>
> *Or you somehow summon the strength to keep going, to get your boat out of the rapids to a place of ease so from that vantage point you can rest. Then, with renewed energy, you can support your loved ones along that same easeful path.*
>
> *Which option do you take? Which do you think leads to the most inner freedom?*
>
> *Can you harness the power of taking action even when you are scared, uncertain, or confused?*
>
> *Instead of pushing or resisting or retreating, can you lovingly support yourself to carry on?*
>
> *Can you nourish the soil of your being so you blossom?*
>
> *Self-nourishment is necessary on this journey down the river of life. Fill your cup so you can overflow. This will allow you to maintain your Willing energy in your loving, your activism, and your life.*
>
> *Visualize holding hands with your confusion and your clarity. Now let's consciously scout the landscape of the Willing self.*

Listen to the audio for this visualization at wildwillingwise.com/willing.

Jot down any quick insights or questions from your visualization.

WILLING MUSINGS

Here are some of the ways you might have diminished or declined your Willing. Put an *X* next to the ones that resonate with you.

_____Always taking responsibility for everything and everyone

_____Demanding others baby you so you feel safe

_____Thinking being Willing means always saying yes

_____Avoiding hurting others or being hurt by not being available

_____Being controlling and judgmental and claiming you are in your clarity

_____Claiming your pleasing and subtle manipulation is empathy or just the way you are

_____Confusing being resistant with taking mindful action

_____Confusing grinding down into constant work with being "productive"

_____Using being a nourisher, creative maven, or martyr for approval or to avoid rejection

_____Closing off your creativity as unimportant or a distraction

Use your tender gardener heart to look at the *X*s on your list above and craft one new agreement that would increase rather than deplete your Willing.

Examples:

I can be productive and soft, steady and receptive.

My willingness to make mistakes or be awkward is my superpower.

I can be nourished and held by others even while I am giving.

My new Willing Energy Agreement: _____

_____

_____

_____

_____

_____

_____

_____

_____

_____

_____

_____

_____

_____

_____

_____

_____

_____

_____

_____

_____

_____

_____

_____

_____

_____

_____

_____

_____

_____

_____

_____

WILLINGNESS TO GIVE AND RECEIVE

All humans have the capacity to nourish and be nourished, to be brave and be vulnerable, to create and to compost. Giving *and* receiving is our human heart beating in rhythm with life. It is literally how we sustain life. Connected to our Willing self and tending to ourselves as well as others, we can do impossible, scary, daunting things.

Can you feel this nourishing and resilient Willing energy within you?

Willing Qualities
Creative
Nurturing
Steady
Sustained
Generous
Generative
Loving
Capable
Adaptive

Which quality resonates with you right now? Pick one from the list above or choose you own. Now, claim it in writing.

I claim being _____.

Think of a recent uncomfortable situation. How did you respond to it?

_____
_____
_____
_____
_____
_____

_____

_____

_____

_____

_____

_____

_____

_____

_____

_____

_____

_____

_____

_____

_____

_____

_____

_____

_____

_____

_____

Now imagine yourself as a seasoned gardener or artist. Tap into the energy of slow and steady. Show up rather than get stuck. Ponder rather than push. Bring in tenderness rather than toughness. Weed and nourish. Play and create. Look intimately for what needs to be supported in your garden and in your art rather than treating everything the same.

Now consider how your response might have been different if you were to draw on the Willing quality you claimed above.

WILLING MEDICINE

Actions to awaken your WILLING when you are stuck . . .

Check the ones that appeal to you.

_____Go outside and jump energetically from rock to rock, puddle to puddle, or high place to low place over and over again.

_____Write a you-are-brave letter to yourself and put it in the mail.

_____Take a workshop or art class that teaches you steady, patient creation.

_____Finger-paint with your toes.

_____Make something with your hands that you've never done before: a quiche, a cardboard box office, a clay sculpture.

_____Curl up in a ball, maybe tightly wrapped in a blanket. Play Bach or Beethoven. As the energy in the music builds, use it to help you poke a finger, then a leg out of your protective ball. Then roll around the floor and dramatically free yourself from the blanket.

_____Read memoirs of other brave beings.

_____Go to an antique store, graveyard, or park and wander. Remind yourself: *My ancestors survived. My ancestors were resilient. My ancestors were willing.**

_____Listen to what message your ancestors have to fuel you forward.

_____Drink a cup of coffee, write down three small things you are going to do today, and take a teeny nap. When you wake up, don't think; just do the three things.

---

* Your ancestors may have been broken, deeply wounded, or neglectful. Or you may not know who your ancestors are. No worries. Call in their strength and lessons separate from their wounds. Know that they are in your blood and bones, even if you don't know where your ancestors' bones and blood arose from.

_____Watch an inspiring, romantic, or sci-fi movie and act out one or more of the most transformed characters; you can even download the script and dress up.

Brainstorm three more ways that you can awaken your Willing energy:

1. _____

2. _____

3. _____

ACTIONS TO REBALANCE YOUR WILLING WHEN YOU ARE BURNT OUT

Check the ones that appeal to you.

_____Raise your arms to the sky. Repeat to yourself: *I am open to receiving. I am open to receiving. I am open to receiving.* Breathe in the energy of sunshine, starlight, the cosmos.

_____Plant your feet firmly on the earth, breathing in nourishment through imaginary roots.

_____Sit with a fire and slowly feed kindling, paper, or pine cones to the flames, asking for help and guidance to gather inner fuel.

_____Regularly repeat to yourself: *Other people can handle their own business. I can focus on mine.*

_____Write down all the things that are draining your energy on separate scraps of paper: fears, frustrations, unhealthy relationships, or work situations. Put them in a bowl or box and ask the Divine Mama to help you release what is not yours to carry and to have the courage to act on what is yours to remedy.

_____Set a five-minute timer. Make whiny sounds. Groan or scream. Vent and release your fears or frustrations through your voice without words.

____Delegate one thing a day to someone in your family or at work.

____Drive or walk to a place that fills your heart and slowly savor.

____Practice these three phases: *I don't know. What do you think? I trust you.*

____Get together with your besties (in person or virtually) and share what you love about each other.

Brainstorm three more ways that you can balance your Willing energy:

1. _____

2. _____

3. _____

What name would you give to your Willing guide? It can be anything at all. Just let it come to you without thinking too much (and of course, be willing to change its name at any time!).

My Willing name is: _____.

BONUS: Create a Willing jar. Write down your favorite suggestions from the list above on separate pieces of paper, fold them up, and place them in the jar. If you are feeling creative, decorate and label the jar. When you are needing some Willing medicine, pick one from your jar and just do it!

And don't forget to invite in Willing peeps who want to practice taking brave, sustainable actions with you. Your kids, parents, peers, pets, even strangers will all benefit. Take the risk to be in community.

WILLING REVIEW

- Willing energy sustains you as you take action (hard and expansive ones and easy, steady ones).
- Willingness does not mean constant pleasing or caretaking.
- We can be brave and vulnerable and still give and receive fully.

When you feel out of balance with your Willing:

1. Step back and tap into your Bravery.
2. Nourish your soil: weed out old stories and compost what is not yours to carry.
3. Ask your Willing guide to inform and integrate your next steps.

Before we move on from Willing to hold hands with Wise, look at yourself in the mirror and say, "Thank you." Take a big breath, you brave soul. Appreciate that you have the courage to reconnect to and balance your inner Willing. HIGH FIVE.

You cannot get through a single day
without having an impact
on the world around you.
What you do makes a difference,
and you have to decide what kind
of difference you want to make.

—NIKKI ROWE

WISE

Learn to be quiet enough to
hear the genuine in yourself,
so that you can hear it in others.

—MARIAN WRIGHT EDELMAN

We search for happiness everywhere, but we are like
Tolstoy's fabled beggar who spent his life sitting on a pot
of gold, under him the whole time. Your treasure—your
perfection—is within you already. But to claim it, you must
leave the busy commotion of the mind and abandon the
desires of the ego and enter into the silence of the heart.

—ELIZABETH GILBERT

What came to mind as you read these quotes? Write freely. Allow your wisdom and compassion to flow. _____

_____
_____
_____
_____
_____
_____
_____
_____
_____
_____
_____
_____
_____
_____
_____
_____
_____
_____
_____
_____
_____
_____
_____
_____
_____
_____
_____
_____
_____
_____
_____
_____

STUCK IN MY OWN SELF-RIGHTEOUS STORY

I thought I was so wise.

After two weeks backpacking in Nepal, I had flown to India to meet my father, who was there on business.

It was my summer break after my second year at university. As a sophomore student of international relations and community development, I felt like I understood the problems of the world.

And the problem was my father.

Well, not my father specifically but what my father represented: global corporate capitalism.

We stood on the twenty-fifth floor of the five-star hotel where he was staying. He called me over and said, "Heather, do you see that village below? When I come here, I always get this room."

I stood next to him and looked down, feeling indignant rage rising.

I listed all the ways this was so wrong in my head. He was so wrong. White male lording his wealth over poor people of color. The West coming to the East to take resources and ending up destroying communities. I knew so much more than he did about right and wrong. I knew what it meant to be a good global citizen. He was far from it.

"One day," my dad continued, "I realized that the women had to walk a long way to get water. So I had a well drilled in the village."

In that instance, something shattered within me. All my self-righteous dogma drained out of me and puddled at my feet. I had been so stuck in my story of how the world should be. But while I had been reading in books about the injustices that colonialism had wrought people all over the world, my father had quietly used his resources to create radical, tangible change for a group of people.

It was my first realization that the world was much more nuanced and complicated than the neat and tidy, black-and-white binary of us versus them, good versus bad.

And that I still had a whole lot to learn.

SEEING BEYOND THE SURFACE

After our most intense day rafting the Grand Canyon, my usually quiet and restrained husband started drinking.

After three beers (which was two more than he ever usually drank), I watched him get louder, more carefree, and relaxed.

On the surface, he looked like just another river rat drinking at the end of the day. But I could see beyond the surface, to the wisdom beneath his actions.

All was not as it appeared.

Later, as the Colorado River flowed and churned past our campsite, I held his head. He was vomiting into the damp sand behind a boulder. I sang to him once the heaving subsided. Then I wrapped my arm around his waist and half-carried him to our tent. I tucked him into his sleeping bag and went to help clean up camp.

After everyone else was asleep, I stayed by the river and prayed.

I asked the waters to carry away the tensions, fears, and frustrations of our rafting trip. We were a very diverse group of professional boaters and novices, longtime friends and strangers, come together on one of the most challenging rivers in the world. Petty fights had broken out among our group, hurt feelings and unnamed fears bubbling up from the past and spilling out.

I had been getting caught in wanting everyone to behave "properly." I didn't want the fighting or tension or simmering frustrations. But at some point on the biggest rapid on the river, I felt Death brush her fingers through my hair and whisper in my ear.

Death was kind, gentle, and loving. She didn't take me down into a watery grave, but she let me know with a kiss to the forehead and a wave that she easily could have.

As we pulled the boats onto shore for the night, I vowed to remember the face of Death, and the calm of knowing she was always with me, waiting to bring me into her watery, infinite embrace.

"Spirit of the river," I prayed that night, "help me to live fully, to flow, to feast fully in this fleeting stretch of river."

I could feel how the ancestors had gone before me on this infinite river, and the descendants were following behind. I could curse my ancestors and feel resentful of the love they hadn't given me or the pain they did.

Or I could leave behind the pollution of my unprocessed fears and stagnant emotions for the ones after me to tend to. I could wake up to how fragile and fleeting this life is, to how fast the river moves. We never know when our time will come to be pulled under to join the underground flow of the dead.

So loving my sick, puking beloved was not a burden but a blessing. We were alive. There was still conflict and tension in our little group and miles to go before we were off this river.

But in that moment, I understood: it is all holy.

WISE COMPASSION

Each of us has a story of ignoring our own wisdom, not learning from our mistakes. We all have times, too, where we allowed ourselves to be weighed down by the muck of our past.

Balancing our Wise energy is about knowing what to hold on to and what to let go of.

We honor our insanely hard and wonderful and humbling and heavenly past and the lessons it has taught us. We accept the consequences of our actions and our mistakes with grace and Compassion and are willing to repair, review, and rectify as needed. And we move forward, knowing that we are wiser and intuitively capable of handling whatever comes next. We relax into and ride the waves on the river of life.

We can reach this place of surrender by practicing Compassion.

Compassion is our capacity to love our flaws, own our truth, and trust the ups and downs of this wild-ass journey. Compassion lets us laugh at ourselves and helps us release our attachment to our fixations of where we—or everyone else—should or shouldn't be on the river. True Compassion starts within and radiates out to all beings.

Our first Wise exercise is to tap into our Compassion so we can begin digesting our pain with love. So that we can compost the grief and loss around us. And so that we can use it as food for something new and beautiful. This is how we heal on an ancestral, personal, and planetary level.

WISE VISUALIZATION

Below is a visualization exercise to help you lead with Compassion. You can find an audio recording of this visualization and all of the others in this book at wildwillingwise.com.

Imagine you are packing for an adventurous river trip. You feel extra strong, capable, and ready to take on the world.

You start by packing nutritious food, water, yummy drinks, a sturdy hat, and lightweight clothing that will keep you both cool and protected from the sun. You also want your tent, kitchen setup, and helpful things like bug spray and a great camera. Oh, and toothpaste, towels, and toilet paper. There are lots of things to pack, but very limited space.

You need space for yourself and your guide as well.

Now, imagine if you also packed into your boat (or dragged behind you):

Your story about your ex
Your broken dreams
Your rebellion
Your painful childhood
Your story about always putting yourself last
Your self-rejection
Your sense of always doing things wrong
Your fear of the unknown
Your list of everything you ever did wrong

Take a moment to draw a simple stick figure picture of a boat, your self, and your guide.

Now draw the pile of old stories and unprocessed emotions you are trying to row with. Add in the underwater anchors of punishment and the weight of blame. As a finishing touch, draw three holes in your boat and label them:

I'm not lovable
I'm not good enough
I'm broken

You'll soon see that it doesn't matter how good your map, how great your guide, or how Wise you may be if you are overburdened AND there are frigging holes in your boat.

Look at this waterlogged, heavy, and cumbersome load you drew and imagine what would happen if you hit a rapid or tried to maneuver around a rock.

Unburden yourself, you Wise One. We need you nimble, light, and ready for anything. Let that shit go.

Listen to the audio for this visualization at wildwillingwise.com/wise.

Jot down any quick insights or questions from your visualization.

_____

_____

_____

_____

_____

_____

_____

_____

_____

_____

_____

_____

_____

_____

_____

_____

_____

_____

_____

_____

_____

_____

WISE MUSINGS

Here are some of the ways you might have cut off or clutched down on your Wise. Put an *X* next to ones that resonate with you.

Note: Remember, you're an angel of gratitude. Be gentle with yourself. Don't go all conditional and judgy on yourself now.

_____Attaching to how you think you should be in your own development

_____Demanding others be loving even while you are conditional and immature

_____Thinking being wise means never having feelings

_____Avoiding others hurt or your own hurt by disregarding stories/experiences

_____Being edgy and critical and claiming it is your intuition

_____Claiming your emotional attachment to the past is just the way it is

_____Confusing being detached or dogmatic with being wise

_____Confusing being distracted with being spiritual

_____Using being an elder or having experience or credentials for approval

_____Closing off your gratitude as unimportant or distraction

Use your sage soul to look at the *X*s on your list above and craft one or more new Wise agreements that would help you relax into your flow.

Examples:

I can have wisdom and feel my grief and gratitude fiercely.

I don't need to prove anything to anyone, ever.

Being unconditional includes both clear boundaries and releasing expectations.

Write freely with sweet Compassion. Lead with love.

My new Wise Energy Agreement: _____

_____

_____

_____

_____

_____

_____

_____

_____

_____

_____

_____

_____

_____

_____

_____

_____

_____

_____

_____

_____

_____

WISE FLOW

All beings have access to bone-deep silent knowing of ancestors, rocks, and roots. Connected to our wisdom, we remember the long story, the weaving of the web of which we are one tiny, and treasured, thread.

Can you feel this still, calm, endless flow within you?

Wise Qualities

Visionary
Patient
Accepting
Calm
Compassionate
Open
Intuitive
Present
Integrated

Which quality above resonates with you right now? Pick one from the list or choose your own. Now, claim it in writing.

I claim being _____.

Think of a recent challenging situation. How did you respond to it?

_____
_____
_____
_____
_____
_____

_____

_____

_____

_____

_____

_____

_____

Imagine yourself as a peaceful sage loving the play and pain and pleasure. Step out of your own immediate saga and see the longer story of your human experience. Cultivate unconditional acceptance rather than conditional closure. Hug rather than hate. Let your heart hold the entire history of this planet's creations: dinosaurs, rocks, oceans, births and deaths, eating and being eaten, love and war, cycles upon cycles.

Write how your response might have been different if you were to draw on the Wise quality you picked above. _____

_____

_____

_____

_____

_____

_____

_____

_____

_____

_____

_____

_____

_____

_____

_____

WISE MEDICINE

Actions to awaken your WISE . . .

Check the ones that appeal to you.

_____Go outside and get close to the earth: lean against a tree, lie in the grass, get on your belly and put your hands in a creek.

_____Write a wisdom letter from your future self and put it in the mail.

_____Sketch with your eyes closed.

_____Make something with your hands that encapsulates the lessons you've gleaned from your life: a collage, sculpture, or painting.

_____Build a tree house or a meditation area inside of your house. Create a comfortable place to sit and watch the world whirl around you. Use everything you see as a form of drinking in wisdom through your pores.

_____Read memoirs of other Wise beings.

_____Talk out loud to the trees, animals, flowers, sky, rocks. Listen for the whispers of their reply.

_____Take yourself and a much younger or older friend on an outing. Listen for their wisdom.

_____Open your arms to the sky. Repeat to yourself: *I am Wise and woven into this wondrous world. I am Wise and woven into this wondrous world. I am Wise and woven into this wondrous world.*

_____Breathe in the gifts of the wind, the warmth of sunshine, the healing of water, the steadiness of earth.

_____Go wisdom hunting: wherever you are, ask yourself, *Where is the wisdom here? Or where is there truth here that I haven't noticed before?*

Brainstorm three more ways that you can awaken your Wise energy:

1. _____

2. _____

3. _____

ACTIONS TO REBALANCE YOUR WISE WHEN YOU'RE HOLDING ON TO TOO MUCH

Check the ones that appeal to you.

_____Sit by a creek and place leaves or twigs in the water, naming each thing you are releasing.

_____Move to flowing, fluid music and practice letting go with your body.

_____Write down all the actions that help you flow and find peace: put them in a bowl or box and each day pick one out to do.

_____Write a letter of forgiveness to yourself.

_____Set a five-minute timer. Make sounds of gratitude. Open your throat and vocalize joy without words.

_____Build an altar to your Beloved Dead with pictures, flowers, and candles. Ask them to stay close to you and remind you to live fully.

_____Clean out your attic, basement, or closets and have a garage sale.

_____Drive or walk to a lake and listen with your whole being to the low, soothing sounds of water on the shore.

_____Visit a coffee shop and practice sitting quietly and sipping your tea or coffee with no agenda or thoughts. Visualize your calm oozing out to others.

_____Spend time with a small child or children. Babysit a friend's kid or volunteer at a kindergarten.

Brainstorm three more ways that you can balance your Wise energy:

1. _____

2. _____

3. _____

What name would you give to your Wise guide? It can be anything at all. Just let it come to you without thinking too much (and of course, be willing to change its name at any time!).

My Wise name is: _____.

BONUS: Create a Wise jar. Write down your favorite suggestions from the list above on separate pieces of paper, fold them up, and place them in the jar. If you are feeling creative, decorate and label the jar. When you are needing some Wise medicine, pick one from your jar and just do it! And don't forget to invite in Wise playmates who can be calm and still with you. Your kids, parents, peers, pets, even strangers can all benefit from more presence. Take the risk to just be.

WISE REVIEW

- Wisdom is not just for those who have years under their belts. We need to access the calm wisdom flowing in all beings, including yours.
- Refusing to let go stops your intuition and insight.
- Compassion begins within and gently ripples out in all directions.

When you feel out of balance with your Wise:

1. Be still and tap into your Compassion.
2. Slow down and look at the long story of any stuckness or stagnation.
3. Ask your wisdom to help you surrender to whatever comes next.

To complete our exploration of Wise energy, close your eyes. Say something to yourself from a compassionate, present voice within. Honor how you are integrating and balancing your inner Wise. INHALE. EXHALE. OPEN.

I did then what I knew how to do.
Now that I know better, I do better.

—MAYA ANGELOU

INTEGRATING YOUR WILD, WILLING, AND WISE

Well done, dear ones! This ends our exploration of the three guides on the river of life: Wild, Willing, and Wise. You have scouted your inner territory, gone deep into what it means to be deficient, centered in, and have excess of each energy. You have discovered new ways to lean into the rapids when things get rough and lie back in the sunshine when things are calm. Let's review.

1. Circle three words that, right now, best embody for you the qualities of Wild, Willing, and Wise that you want to hold. Your three words can be from the lists below or you can write your own.

WILD	WILLING	WISE
Curious	Creative	Visionary
Playful	Nurturing	Patient
Experimental	Steady	Accepting
Connected	Sustained	Calm
Wondrous	Generous	Compassionate
Exuberant	Generative	Open
Joyful	Loving	Intuitive
Spontaneous	Capable	Present
Carefree	Adaptive	Integrated

Now bring your three words together in a sentence:

I am _____, _____, and _____.

Examples:

Wild: Curious
Willing: Creative
Wise: Compassionate
I am curious, creative, and compassionate.

Wild: Experimental
Willing: Nurturing
Wise: Present
I am experimental, nurturing, and present.

Wild: Playful
Willing: Steady
Wise: Accepting
I am playful, steady, and accepting.

Write your Wild, Willing, Wise words on a piece of paper or a sticky note and put it someplace you'll see every day. To keep it fresh, review and update your three qualities every three months or so. And always remember, you don't need to go down the Grand Canyon alone in a leaky boat with no paddle. Good guides make everything better. We are all in this together. We are the fucking river.

WE ARE THE RIVER

Below is the final visualization exercise to help you integrate your Wild, Willing, and Wise energies. You can find an audio recording of this visualization and all of the others in this book at wildwillingwise.com.

Imagine being on a river journey with yourself and some fabulous friends. Let it be a wonderfully diverse, Wild, Willing, and Wise crowd: pick someone from your childhood, your favorite grandparent who has been dead for twenty years, your new friend you met a few weeks ago, a favorite musician or inspirational figure from the movies. Feel your sense of play, presence, and purpose as you get ready to start down the river.

But wait—also invite your cranky neighbor, your codependent ex, and your son struggling with addiction.

And don't forget the crying hungry child displaced by war, your unrequited love from college, and the waitress at your favorite restaurant that always seems a little anxious and scared beneath her smile.

Invite them all.

Remember: they are all reflections of you and you of them, facets of life manifesting into a myriad of forms and expressions, ever changing.

At times, you will be generous, courageous, and free; at other times, you will be cranky, anxious, and scared.

At times, you'll be paddling and giggling with your best friend; at other times, riding the rough rapids with your child struggling with addiction.

Open your heart to it all.

Everyone is on this flowing river.

We are the river: glorious, messy, churning, calm, terrifying, blissful.

Remember: The only way out is through. Don't jump out of the boat. Take it slow. Being an expert is helpful, but it doesn't mean you won't capsize. Good guides make everything better. Surrender to the flow. We are all in this together.

Keep paddling, beloved.

Listen to this final audio visualization at wildwillingwise.com/integrate.

Jot down any quick insights or questions from your visualization.

_____

_____

_____

_____

_____

_____

_____

_____

_____

_____

_____

_____

_____

_____

_____

_____

_____

_____

We're all water from different rivers, that's why it's so easy to meet; we're all water in this vast, vast ocean, someday we'll evaporate together.

—YOKO ONO

BONUS! WARRIOR HEART PRACTICE

You've gained so much in reconnecting with your Wild, Willing, and Wise inner guides, and you may be feeling full and sassy. If so, feel free to skip this bonus Warrior Heart practice and flip to the final love letter and resources sections. (You can always come back to the Bonus section later!)

But if you are feeling ready and excited to learn a specific tool to assist you on heeding the call of your guides, let's dive in!

> To achieve the mood of a warrior
> is not a simple matter. It is a revolution.
> To regard the lion and the water rats
> and our fellow humans as equals
> is a magnificent act of a warrior's spirit.
> It takes power to do that.
>
> **—CARLOS CASTANEDA**

The warrior who is impelled by love
is a far greater warrior than
one who is driven by anger.

—THÍCH NHẤT HẠNH

What came to mind as you read these quotes? Write freely with a brave
heart. _____

_____
_____
_____
_____
_____
_____
_____
_____
_____
_____
_____
_____
_____
_____
_____
_____
_____
_____
_____
_____
_____

WARRIOR HEART PRACTICE

As we've learned throughout *Wild, Willing, and Wise*, we must unburden ourselves so we are light, nimble, and ready for anything that the river of life throws at us. But that does NOT mean:

1. Chucking everything overboard, finding someone else to fix the holes, and then rowing merrily, merrily, merrily down the stream; or
2. Exploring endlessly how we got all these holes in our boat, every hurt, every wrong, every trauma, and then expecting we'll be awarded a brand-new boat.

Unburdening yourself is actually much, much easier. It is really about learning to look at what appear to be your burdens as your blessings.

Enter the Warrior Heart practice.

The Warrior of the Heart has the courage, patience, and perseverance to know when and what to fight for, and when to rest. She consciously acts from respect and love, knows how to move through and with any obstacle, and learns from her mistakes. She intimately understands how everything is interconnected and interdependent.

The Warrior of the Heart knows how to take what appear to be burdens and alchemize them into blessings. Her skill and her practice is untangling old feelings and stories so that she can intentionally harness her Wild, Willing, and Wise energies for any given situation.

In this bonus section, I share one of my all-time favorite practices for preparing yourself for battle—in this case, the battle for your energy and intent. This practice is a modified version of the one that appears in my book *The Warrior Heart Practice*.

The Warrior Heart practice is a straightforward and well-tested system that will help you untangle your emotions from your stories and your stories from the truth, then connect the truth with your intent.

In the Warrior Heart practice, you will learn how to move through a simple process that transforms confusion into clarity and pain into peace.

Feeling, Story, Truth, Intent: These are the four chambers of the Warrior Heart practice, which change the way you operate in the world by helping you to rearrange the pieces of your personal puzzles into an integrated new whole—mentally, emotionally, and physically.

WARRIOR UNTANGLING

If we keep trying to control or ignore our emotions and reactions, they go beneath the surface, waiting. And these old emotions and hidden stories have a tendency to stink up the waters, especially when they are then held down by shame, blame, and guilt. They may start as tiny threads of annoyance or hurt, but they are all too easily tangled up in far older, even ancestral, lines of past pain.

Sometimes, they are so tangled up in our way of being that we can't access our Wild, Willing, and Wise guides. Even when we know which energies are out of balance and what we need to tap into, we are so trapped in these old hurts that we can't break through. First, we must dive down deep into the cold waters of our history to undo these old personal, family, cultural, and generational knots.

Here is a real-time example of how I used the Warrior Heart practice to help me find my way out of the twisted chaos of my past pain after being rocked by an unexpected wave of emotion.

Now, this example is not Grand Canyon dramatic. In fact, it is a simple, everyday rocky-water sort of problem. But it is in learning how to navigate the smaller ripples of hurt that give us the energy, and skill, to turn toward the bigger waves of old woundings and pain.

Imagine this with me:

I just finished responding to a challenging email from a business partner, and I notice I feel edgy, teary, and generally discombobulated. I notice wisps of story floating through my head: worry about money, fear I'm going to be somehow betrayed, exhaustion.

I am aware of my feelings and thoughts as I make my morning coffee, wash dishes, and answer other emails, but I can't make sense of why I am feeling so out of sorts.

I could go on with my day and let my attention be hooked by other projects and tasks. And I also know if I don't clear the sticky, churning emotions and story in my being, they will mostly likely sink into the murky waters below my consciousness and stagnate.

So I pause.

With pen and paper nearby, I close my eyes and, one at a time, I travel into the four chambers of the Warrior Heart practice: Feeling, Story, Truth, and Intent.

WILD FEELINGS

In the Warrior Heart practice, we start in the Feeling Chamber, which is the realm of our Wild. The practice is to simply feel our emotions, **without trying to understand, fix, control, or explain**.

Here I ask my Wild self to help me be with and breathe into my emotions.

The question I ask myself is simple: "What am I feeling?"

FEELINGS: Fear in my chest, constriction, wanting to curl in and protect, exhaustion, grief.

Breathe. Feel. There is nothing to do, and the practice is to stay out of the story and simply be with the emotion in a gentle, aware, present way.

I sit with my discomfort and say to myself, "I'm here. Hi. It's okay to feel the way you feel. There is nothing you need to do or feel or be."

After breathing and being with my emotions and noticing where they are in my body, I imagine walking to the second chamber of my heart, the Story Chamber.

WILD STORIES

In the Story Chamber, we explore the wild, runaway stories that are giving rise to our Wild feelings. What are the rocks and currents that are causing the churning waters of our emotional reaction? We dive deep beneath the emotions to the underlying story. This means not editing, trying to make the story nicer or kinder, or shaping the story in any way.

The question I ask in the Story Chamber is, "What stories are in my head?"

I brain-dump what is actually in my head. I let all the messy, tangled storylines emerge. In the writing below, you'll see I start off writing what I was thinking in first person and then shift to the voice of my judge, which I realized was speaking to me in second person.

STORY: I'm being set up to fail, and I'm going to be abandoned. I'm putting so much energy into this project, and what if it fails? What if I can't bring people together the way I want to and the fighting and separation continues and is actually irreparable?

You are going to fail: you are not doing it right. Nobody wants to help you, and you are just full of yourself for thinking you can fix something that is so broken.

I write without thinking, letting myself go deeper into the story to explore everything that has been tangled together—without judgment or trying to make it nicer or prettier or more spiritual. I let myself be in the mucky mess of the story.

Once I explore the stories I am telling myself (knowing that I don't need to understand, fix, change, defend, justify, or repress), my next step is to get to the truth and set new intent.

WILLING TRUTH

The next two chambers are the realm of Willing. Now that we have named our stories, we can step beyond them to scout for the truth and make new choices. It's time to call in our nourishing, sustaining energy to stand with us.

Two things I've learned about getting to the truth:

One, the truth is really simple. No more than one sentence. If you start justifying, blaming, feeling ashamed, or telling another story, it is not truth.

Two, it will resonate in your body as true. You'll feel a sense of relaxation or openness when you name the truth. And sometimes you'll also find while you don't like the truth, it is a relief to know what is true for you, or in a particular situation.

The question I ask myself to start this part of the process is: "What is actually true here? What do I know is true?"

TRUTH: I'm doing my best and it may or may not work out.

Now, my truth may have been "I don't want to do this anymore." Or "I need more support." Or "This is not mine to untangle." And more truth may arise over the next few days. Separating out our emotions, story, and truth creates space for healing, compassionate understanding of self and others . . . and new, intentional action.

WILLING INTENT

The fourth chamber, Intent, helps us to create a focus for what's next.

Your intent will be one word and is the answer to the question: "Where do I want to put my focus in relationship to this situation?"

Just like I did in the Truth Chamber, I open myself to new possibilities.

INTENT: Faith.

I want to trust the process I'm involved with in the community I'm working with. I want to be willing to stay in when things get hard. I also want to have the faith to know when it is time to step out.

Whatever your intent is—Peace, Joy, Healing, Courage, Truth, Vision, Love, Banana—it doesn't have to make sense to anyone else, it only needs to resonate with your being and help you make wise, compassionate choices going forward.

And now I that have sat with my Wild feelings and stories and Willed my truth and intent into being, it is time to call in my Wise.

CIRCLING BACK

The next step in the Warrior Heart practice is courting the realm of calm witnessing. We call in our wisdom to help us free up the flow.

I bring together my intent—Faith—and my truth—*I'm doing my best, and it may or may not work out.*

Then I imagine walking back into the Story Chamber. The fears and self-doubt that are holding my story together start to dissolve in the waters of my intent and my truth.

There is not a specific thing you are trying to do in the Story Chamber as you circle back. Sometimes the story completely unravels as you bring it back into your loving gaze. Other times you will see that it is a much more tangled story from childhood or a more recent painful experience. When we bring the wisdom of our intent and truth back to our story, we bring in our story-unknotting superpowers of patience and presence.

NEW STORY: It may not work out, and I may fail. This is a learning experience, and I am not in control of how others respond and react. I hold compassion for the part of me that wants to do everything perfectly and for the part of me that is afraid of being abandoned. I'm willing to take risks and try new things and know it may or may not work. And it could be fun or beautiful or wonderfully successful as well!

We don't curse our boat or feel guilty for having too much weight. Here, we show the same Wise compassion for ourselves. We know it is going to take time and effort to get free, and we lovingly get to work.

Next, we retrace our steps to end where we began: in the Feeling Chamber.

Again, there is nothing to do or fix, just witness and somatically be with what you are feeling. There is no right or wrong; the point is actually not to feel absolutely clear and clean and be without emotions. The point is to be truthful with where you are and what you are feeling now.

I hang out in the Feeling Chamber for a bit, connecting with my body and breath, getting present in this moment and time.

NEW FEELING: Calm. Open and curious. Some tension in my upper chest, just under my collarbone.

Sometimes you will feel spaciousness and peace; other times you may feel that the mud of your emotions has been stirred up. Just be with everything. You can always come back later and do the Warrior Heart practice again to help continue to clear the debris.

Here's the cool part about something like the Warrior Heart practice: once we untangle our feelings and stories, our natural curiosity (Wild), sustaining energy (Willing), and embodied intuition (Wise) arise naturally. We rest in the sacred boat of our truth and inner peace, with a more solid container to navigate any coming rapids.

The next section is a guided exercise to take you gently through the Warrior Heart practice. If this practice resonates with you, I encourage you to go deeper and read *The Warrior Heart Practice*.

WARRIOR MEDICINE

When you find yourself paddling in hellish circles of addictions, destructive habits, and procrastination; drowning in your frustration, hurt, or rage at someone's actions or behavior; or terrified at what rapids may lie ahead, remember you are a Warrior of the Heart and you can untangle that mess of feelings and Stories holding you back and claim a new truth and intention.

Here's how.

Get your journal if you want, or sit, walk, dance as you do the Warrior Heart practice. There is no one right way!

BE WILD

Notice when you are triggered, in reaction, afraid, stuck in a pattern, or just a wee bit off-kilter.

Enter the Feeling Chamber. What emotions are you experiencing? What are you feeling in your body? _____

_____

_____

_____

_____

_____

_____

Just be with your feelings. Breathe.

You may feel like you are being sucked into a hole, getting tossed about by crashing waves, or being beaten against rocks. Let go into the turbulent waters of your emotions.

Now, walk toward the Story Chamber. What are you telling yourself? What stories do you have in your head? _____

_____

_____

_____

_____

_____

_____

Give yourself permission to witness the whole fucking tangled mess without judgment. Breathe.

BE WILLING

Next, go to the Truth Chamber.

What is actually true here? _____

_____

_____

_____

_____

_____

_____

_____

_____

Bravely listen for the bell of your truth ringing through your body. One sentence. Simple. Allow space for more or different truths to arise as you integrate this practice.

Last, enter the Intent Chamber.

Where do I want to put my focus in relationship to this situation?

Pick one word that encapsulates your intent.

My intent is _____.

BE WISE

Now you'll circle back through the Intent, Truth, and Story Chambers.

Imagine bringing your word from the Intent Chamber into the Truth Chamber and then stepping back into the Story Chamber with a new Wise perspective.

I bring my intent _____ and my truth _____ back into the Story Chamber to see with new eyes and an open heart.

What do I now see or know in regard to my story? _____

_____

_____

_____

_____

_____

_____

_____

_____

_____

_____

_____

_____

_____

_____

_____

_____

_____

_____

_____

Be curious, but don't try to fix or make anything specific happen. Bring your Wise patience and long-story perspective into the story that you are untangling and wait for insight or understanding.

FINAL DESTINATION: THE FEELING CHAMBER

Close your Warrior Heart practice by stepping back into the Feeling Chamber and noticing from that Wise and peaceful witness place how you feel. There is no right or wrong answer here, just the truth of what is happening in your emotional body.

What am I feeling now? What do I sense in my body? _____

_____

_____

_____

_____

_____

_____

_____

_____

_____

_____

_____

_____

_____

_____

_____

_____

_____

_____

_____

_____

Once you have completed the full practice, go for a short walk or drink some water, then come back and journal any insights that arose. Below are some prompts:

Is there a much older or more tangled story that I need to untangle?

How can I remind myself about my intent and truth when I am in the same or a similar situation?

Where could I use more support?

Which guide do I feel most called toward now: Wild, Willing, or Wise?

_____

_____

_____

_____

_____

_____

_____

_____

_____

_____

_____

_____

_____

_____

_____

_____

Listen to the audio for the visualization of the Warrior Heart practice at wildwillingwise.com/warrior.

WARRIOR REVIEW

Being a Warrior of the Heart is not about how strong and independent you are but how resourceful and light you can be.

Releasing emotional and mental baggage takes warrior courage and commitment.

The Warrior Heart practice is a potent tool for untangling from old feelings and stories and embracing a new truth and intent.

When you are feeling stuck in a tangle of old stories and hurts:

1. Let go of blame, shame, and guilt and ask yourself: What would a Warrior of the Heart do?
2. Set aside time to do the Warrior Heart practice.
3. Start with the smaller ripples of hurt before you turn toward the bigger waves of old woundings and pain.

Any great warrior is also a scholar, and a poet, and an artist.

—STEVEN SEAGAL

A FINAL LOVE LETTER

Dearest Spectacular Being,

Hi, it's me, your Future Self.
I see the Wild, Willing, Wise warrior that you are.
I see how you are growing and changing and learning.
I see where you are struggling, floundering, forcing.
I see what you are carrying and what you have released.
In case you need some cheerleading or a little reminder:
I give you permission to be Wildly silly, carefree, and playfully aware of what delights you.
I give you permission to be Willingly open, steady, and courageously creative in the challenges and in the flow.
I give you permission to be Wisely present, grateful, and compassionate with yourself and all beings.
I give you permission to own your Warrior Heart without blame, shame, or guilt.
Know that your future self is not someplace in the distance, unreachable and unattainable.
I'm right here, guiding you every step of the way.
Don't jump out of the boat, sweetheart.
You've already arrived.
And you've just begun.
I'm with you.

With love,
Your Future Self

RESOURCES

VISUALIZATIONS

Visualization #1: *Pick a guide:* wildwillingwise.com/guide, p. 42.

Visualization #2: *Wild:* wildwillingwise.com/wild, p. 57.

Visualization #3: *Willing:* wildwillingwise.com/willing, p. 79.

Visualization #4: *Wise:* wildwillingwise.com/wise, p. 99.

Visualization #5: *Integrate:* wildwillingwise.com/integrate, p. 114.

Visualization #6: *Warrior:* wildwillingwise.com/warrior, p. 135.

GODDESSES AND GODS AND MYTHICAL BEINGS, OH MY

Here are examples of different deities and mythical and human beings around the world that show us the Wild, Willing, and Wise ways.

WILD	WILLING	WISE
Artemis	Isis	Hecate
Sarasvati	Oshun	Kali
Pele	Kuan Yin	Baba Yaga
Kama	Parvati	Spider Woman
Pan	Jesus	Odin
Dionysus	Gandhi	Athena
Miley Cyrus	Mother Teresa	Jane Goodall

Who would you add to these lists of guides (public figures or from your personal life)? _____

_____

_____

_____

_____

_____

_____

_____

_____

_____

_____

_____

_____

_____

_____

_____

NOTES

IF YOU RESONATED WITH **WILD, WILLING, AND WISE**
AND ENJOYED **THE WARRIOR HEART PRACTICE BONUS,**
JOIN ME IN GOING DEEPER BY READING
THE WARRIOR HEART PRACTICE,
ALSO PUBLISHED BY ST. MARTIN'S ESSENTIALS.

A Simple Process to
Transform Confusion into Clarity
and Pain into Peace

The
Warrior
Heart
Practice

HEATHERASH AMARA
Author of *Warrior Goddess Training*

Dive into the following excerpt of the first two chapters of *The Warrior Heart Practice.*

FROM THE PREFACE OF WARRIOR HEART PRACTICE: YOUR INNER BEACON OF LIGHT

No matter how much you have suffered or how much you suffer now, whether you feel slightly dissatisfied or completely lost and confused, there is a light illuminating your way if you only look for it with new eyes. The purpose of this book is to remind you that a beacon of light constantly shines within you like a lighthouse on the coast, guiding you away from the familiar but rocky shores of struggle, stress, and suffering, and showing you the way toward the true harbor of your innate integrity and peace.

The current waters in which we live are turbulent, unpredictable, and filled with fears of not being or doing "enough." If you suffer from a troubling lack of confidence and a bounty of self-judgment despite your successes, if you feel unfulfilled in your relationships or work, or if you have a nagging sense that there is something vital missing within, then you are living within the shallow waters of who you think you are supposed to be rather than from the nourishing depth of who you truly are.

While the pure light of your being is always shining, it can and does get buried beneath years of trying to please other people, an accumulation of hurts, and life's daily demands. Silence underlies all sound, whether it is a whisper or a pounding wave. In the middle of a raging storm, the underlying stillness is overwhelmed, but it is still there, ready to be accessed at any time. Beneath the choppy waves of your mind and the crashing loudness of fearful emotions lie the silent depths of your authentic expression.

The Warrior Heart Practice shares a pathway to support you in moving beneath your mental and emotional noise so that you can immerse yourself in the inspiration and stillness within you. This book will show you how to move beyond the struggles of everyday life where we often seek outside approval, and how to be less serious and more ecstatic on your healing, work, or spiritual path. It offers tools for finding ease and flow rather than struggle in your relationships and how to be more grounded, present, and playful.

The question is not "Is it really possible to live from my authenticity and heart?" but rather "How do I free myself from the mental prison of judgment, comparison, self-criticism, and worry to create a life built on true acceptance, unshakable inner joy, and bountiful trust? How do I find and sustain connection to the profound creative brilliance and capacity that lie within the core of my being?"

The truth is you are a magnificent, nuclear-bomb force of love and potential. And if you've had enough of playing small and judging yourself into scattered, itty-bitty pieces of who you really are, this book will awaken the warrior within that you need to claim who you are really meant to be.

This book is a bridge and the cleansing waters flowing beneath it simultaneously. The Warrior Heart's big-picture view will help you accept and integrate all the parts of you so that you are once again connected to your creative, inspired inner wisdom. The specific method of the Warrior Heart practice is like a power washer that will wash away the debris that has accumulated and clouded your authentic knowing.

Within these pages, you will learn how to celebrate both your divine nature and your quirky personality, while balancing practical action with spiritual inspiration.

I'm excited to be on this journey with you.

To get the most out of this book, I recommend that you read each of the chapters, getting an overview of the teachings and the different chambers. Skip over the exercises and questions for later. Then come back and review each chapter, adding in the exercises and questions. You don't have to do every exercise; you may start out by doing one per chapter or picking the exercises or questions that most speak to you.

If you are ready to jump in and want to go deep quickly, make sure you have a journal specifically for the Warrior Heart practice. Read chapter 1, answer the questions at the end of the chapter, and then print out several of the Warrior Heart practice sheets at the end of chapter 2 that you can use for specific issues as they arise. At the end of each chapter, review and answer the questions, and do each of the exercises.

The Warrior Heart practice is a simple sequential process; through the coming chapters, I will take you step-by-step through how to find your truth and view your story in a totally different way. While there is no right way to use the book, I do recommend that you get to know each of the different chambers and do them in order as you learn the practice. Then as you get more adept, you can begin to improvise and use the chambers in a way that best serves where you are.

Before we get into the map and method of the practice, let me introduce myself and how the Warrior Heart teachings came to be.

FROM THE INTRODUCTION

In 1973, my parents brought my sister and me to India. We went as tourists with the intent of touching the luminous beauty of the Taj Mahal and to be touched by the immense contrasts of poverty, chaos, devotion, and peace that pervade India. I was seven years old.

Earlier that year, I had decided to write a book, but when I sat down to start my bestseller, a sudden insight gave me pause. Sitting there at my wooden desk with my pad of lavender paper and my favorite black felt-tip pen in hand, I realized I was missing one crucial ingredient to be an author:

Experience.

So I put away my paper and pen and went outside to play. I trusted implicitly that what I needed to write for my book would come. Many experiences, which I would eventually write about, began a few months later with a life-altering, four-second event.

The catalyst for this awakening came wrapped in the package of an Indian child who was about my age. I saw her as I was walking down a dusty New Delhi street while I was holding my dad's hand. I remember the heavy, sticky heat, looking down, and worrying that my white sandals were going to get dirty. When I looked back up, I suddenly locked eyes with this young Indian girl walking toward me.

She was barefoot, draped in a soiled fragment of a dress that wrapped around an all-elbows-and-knees frame. I almost looked away, embarrassed by my clean dress, shiny shoes, and full belly. But as we came closer, our gaze became even more connected. Everything around me stopped. The noise of the traffic dissolved. The fear I hadn't realized I was holding simply evaporated.

As I looked deeply into her brown eyes, a warm sun radiated out from her heart. Every cell in my being smiled in utter happiness, and as this occurred, she reflected the same utter happiness and recognition in her smile back to me.

I felt as if I had reunited with my best friend after many long years of separation. This feeling did not dissolve after she had passed; it only grew stronger. I was ecstatic. I felt like I'd been dipped in liquid beauty. Everything around me became a sweet song that I suddenly remembered how to sing.

What I learned in that seconds-long merging, which I've forgotten and re-remembered many times since that day, is that within each of us resides a clear pool of peace and an unbreakable core connection, regardless of our circumstances. The state I felt in those four seconds was the awakening of my authentic Warrior Heart.

Authenticity is the state of being undivided, in integrity, and clear. When we are in wholeness, we are rooted in our truest nature, and we live our lives from a conscious and clear place of faith in ourselves and the wisdom of our Warrior Heart. We learn to navigate our challenges with more and more grace, faith, and presence.

Like my experience with the girl in India, all of us have those precious moments or days of connection and openhearted abiding love for life. We touch this state when we fall in love, hold a baby, or achieve a longtime goal. But when our happiness or self-worth is tied to a moment, person, or place rather than anchored in our being as our authentic Warrior Heart expression, it is frustratingly fleeting and transitory. It takes tools and practice to stabilize this state of inner joy that is independent from our external experience.

ABOUT THE AUTHOR

HeatherAsh Amara is an author, mentor, land steward, philanthropist, and lover of fire who has spent the last three decades weaving together earth-based wisdom, mindfulness, and practical strategies for creative, courageous, and compassionate change.

HeatherAsh has written nine books and created numerous audio projects, including the bestseller *Warrior Goddess Training* (Hierophant Publishing, 2014), *The Seven Secrets to Healthy, Happy Relationships* with don Miguel Ruiz Jr. (Hierophant Publishing, 2017), *The Art of Listening* audiobook (Sounds True, 2016), and *The Warrior Heart Practice* (St. Martin's Essentials, 2020). She is the founder of the Center for Creative Intent, which offers space and education for leaders to retreat, learn, and grow their capacity for leading their communities through the transitions and contradictions we all face.

When she's home, HeatherAsh plants her feet in New Mexico, but as a lifelong nomad, she spends most of her time traveling, teaching, and writing in cafés around the world.

ACKNOWLEDGMENTS

Gratitude to the waterfall outside of the house in the Catskills where I write in each January.

Gratitude to the creek that flows through the land I love and steward in northern New Mexico.

Gratitude to the August rains that helped some of the trees survive after the wildfire.

Gratitude to the sea that separates the Outer Hebrides from mainland Scotland, where I cried on the ferry as I traveled for the first time to the land of my maternal ancestors.

Gratitude to the wild rapids of delight, the willing tears of joy and sorrow, the wise ocean depths.

Gratitude to the water that connects us all.

INDEX